THE ESSENTIAL CBT GUIDE FOR PARENTS

Building Strong Bonds using Evidence-Based Strategies and Tools for Meaningful Parent-Child Relationships through CBT

Maxine D. Condon

ABOUT THE AUTHOR

 Maxine D Condon in her early 50s is an author from the United States. She is best known for her books on psychology, emotions, and self-help therapy.

Maxine D Condon was born in 1973 in a small town in the Midwest. She grew up in a family that valued education, so she knew from an early age that she wanted to pursue a career in the field.

Maxine went on to pursue a degree in psychology from a local college. After graduation she immediately began working as a clinical psychologist, helping people with various mental health issues. She quickly rose to prominence in her field and was soon invited to speak at conferences and seminars across the country.

Maxine's career quickly blossomed and she went on to write more books on the topics of psychology and emotions. She also wrote cookbooks and diet plans to help people manage conditions such as heart disease.

Maxine is now a well-known author and speaker. She has appeared on television programs and talk shows and her books have been featured in prominent publications. She is also a regular contributor to various magazines and blogs.

Maxine D Condon is a passionate advocate for mental health and wellbeing. She is passionate about helping people understand and manage their emotions and find the joy in life her mission is to help others find the courage to take control of their lives and to live with confidence and purpose.

Table of Contents

INTRODUCTION

Sarah, a dedicated and loving parent, found herself constantly grappling with the complexities of raising her two children, Emily and Alex. Despite her best efforts, she often felt at a loss when it came to managing their behavior and fostering healthy communication.

One fortunate day, fate led Sarah to stumble upon a book that promised to be a game-changer: "Unlocking Parenting Success with CBT". Eager for a solution, she eagerly delved into its pages. As Sarah embarked on her journey through the book's insightful guidance, she discovered the power of Cognitive Behavioral Therapy (CBT) in transforming her parenting approach.

She learned to identify negative thought patterns and reframe them into positive ones, allowing her to respond more effectively to her children's needs.

Equipped with evidence-based strategies, Sarah began implementing active listening techniques and validating her children's emotions. Through assertive communication and setting boundaries, she fostered an atmosphere of trust and respect. Sarah also discovered the importance of teaching emotional intelligence, helping Emily and Alex navigate their feelings with grace and understanding.

The book's practical exercises proved invaluable, as Sarah found herself engaging in collaborative problem-solving activities and nurturing creativity through art therapy. As her newfound skills took root, she witnessed a blossoming connection with her children, built on a foundation of love and mutual understanding Over time, Sarah noticed remarkable changes in her family dynamics. Tantrums decreased, replaced by open discussions and constructive conflict resolution. Anxiety and stress no longer held her children captive, as they gained tools to manage their emotions effectively.

Through the transformative journey offered by the CBT guide, Sarah evolved into a confident, resilient parent. She witnessed the profound impact her newfound skills had on her children's well-being and self-esteem. The once-rocky path of parenthood had transformed into a harmonious and joyful journey, filled with shared laughter, growth, and unwavering bonds.

Sarah's story serves as a reminder that with the right knowledge and tools, even the most daunting parenting challenges can be overcome. Through her dedication and the invaluable guidance of the CBT book, she created a nurturing environment where her children thrived, forever grateful for the parent who sought out solutions and embraced the transformative power of change.

CHAPTER 1

UNDERSTANDING THE POWER OF CBT IN PARENTING

1.1 What is Cognitive Behavioral Therapy (CBT)?

In cognitive behavioral therapy (CBT), the relationship between thoughts, emotions, and behaviors is the main focus of treatment. It is a widely recognized and evidence-based approach used to address a variety of mental health issues, including anxiety disorders, depression, phobias, addiction, and more.

CBT operates on the principle that our thoughts and perceptions about ourselves, others, and the world around us greatly influence our emotions and behaviors.

It emphasizes that distorted or negative thinking patterns can contribute to emotional distress and maladaptive behaviors.

The goal of CBT is to identify and modify unhelpful thoughts and behaviors to alleviate psychological distress and promote positive change. It involves a collaborative process between the therapist and the individual, where they work together to challenge negative beliefs, develop healthier thinking patterns, and implement effective coping strategies.

CBT incorporates various techniques and interventions tailored to the individual's specific needs. These may include cognitive restructuring, which involves challenging and reframing negative thoughts, and behavioral activation, which encourages engagement in positive activities to improve mood. Other techniques, such as relaxation training, problem-solving skills, exposure therapy, and social skills training, can also be utilized within the CBT framework.

One of the strengths of CBT is its focus on the present and its practical, goal-oriented nature. It helps individuals develop skills and strategies they can apply in their daily lives to manage distressing thoughts and emotions effectively. CBT is typically a short-term therapy, but its effects can be long-lasting, empowering individuals to become their agents of change. It's important to note that while CBT is highly effective for many people, it may not be the best approach for everyone or all mental health conditions. Consulting with a qualified mental health professional is recommended to determine the most appropriate treatment approach for individual needs.

1.2 How CBT Benefits Parent-Child Relationships

Cognitive Behavioral Therapy (CBT) can offer several benefits to your parent-child relationship by providing you with valuable skills and strategies to foster healthier communication, understanding, and connection.

Here are some ways CBT can benefit your parent-child relationship:

1. **Improved Communication:** CBT teaches effective communication techniques, such as active listening and assertive communication. These skills can enhance your ability to understand your child's needs, validate their emotions, and express yourself clearly and respectfully. Improved communication can lead to better understanding and stronger bonds between you and your child.

2. **Enhanced Emotional Regulation:** CBT equips both parents and children with tools to manage and regulate their emotions effectively. By understanding the connection between thoughts, emotions, and behaviors, you can help your child identify and cope with their emotions in healthy ways. This promotes emotional resilience and reduces conflicts that may arise from emotional dysregulation.

3. **Constructive Problem-Solving:** CBT emphasizes problem-solving skills, which can be applied to parenting challenges. By teaching your child how to identify problems, brainstorm solutions, and evaluate the pros and cons of different options, you empower them to take an active role in finding resolutions. This collaborative approach fosters a sense of autonomy and builds problem-solving skills that benefit both the parent and child.

4. **Positive Reinforcement and Encouragement:** CBT encourages the use of positive reinforcement to acknowledge and reinforce desired behaviors in children. By focusing on their strengths and efforts, you can boost their self-esteem and motivation. Positive reinforcement also helps create a nurturing and supportive environment, reinforcing the parent-child bond.

5. **Modeling Healthy Coping Strategies:** As a parent, you play a crucial role in modeling behaviors and coping strategies for your child. Through CBT, you can develop effective coping skills for yourself, such as stress management techniques or adaptive thinking patterns. By demonstrating these skills in your own life, you provide your child with valuable examples of healthy ways to cope with challenges.

6. **Strengthening Empathy and Understanding:** CBT promotes empathy and understanding by encouraging parents to see situations from their child's perspective. By recognizing and validating their emotions, you can create an atmosphere of empathy, which strengthens the parent-child connection and promotes a sense of emotional safety and trust.

By integrating CBT principles and techniques into your parenting approach, you can create a more supportive, empathetic, and communicative environment. This fosters a stronger parent-child relationship, enhances your child's emotional well-being, and equips both of you with the skills to navigate challenges together.

1.3 The Role of CBT in Building Strong Bonds

The role of Cognitive Behavioral Therapy (CBT) in building strong bonds between parents and children is significant. CBT offers several key elements that contribute to the development of a healthy and nurturing parent-child relationship:

1. Improved Communication: Effective communication is vital for building strong bonds. CBT provides parents with essential skills, such as active listening, assertive communication, and validation. These techniques foster open and empathetic communication, allowing parents to understand their children's thoughts, emotions, and needs better.

2. By promoting clear and respectful dialogue, CBT helps parents and children connect on a deeper level and establish stronger bonds.

3. Emotion Regulation: CBT emphasizes the understanding and management of emotions. Parents who engage in CBT can learn strategies to regulate their own emotions and teach these skills to their children. By modeling healthy emotional regulation techniques, parents create a supportive environment where children feel safe expressing their feelings. This emotional attunement fosters empathy, and understanding, and strengthens the parent-child bond.

4. Challenging Negative Thoughts and Beliefs: CBT focuses on identifying and challenging negative thoughts and beliefs that can impact parent-child relationships. Parents can learn to recognize unhelpful thinking patterns that may lead to misunderstandings or conflicts.

By reframing these thoughts and adopting more positive and realistic perspectives, parents can cultivate a more positive and supportive atmosphere. This shift in thinking can improve interactions, enhance empathy, and strengthen the parent-child bond.

5.   Problem-Solving Skills: CBT equips parents with problem-solving skills that are valuable in navigating the challenges of parenting. By teaching parents how to break down problems into manageable steps, evaluate solutions, and make informed decisions, CBT empowers them to address parenting challenges effectively. These problem-solving skills create a sense of collaboration, mutual respect, and shared decision-making between parents and children, enhancing the parent-child bond.

6.   Building Trust and Security: CBT emphasizes the importance of trust and security in relationships. Through consistent and responsive parenting, parents can create a safe and supportive environment for their children.

By providing clear boundaries, nurturing emotional connection, and addressing their children's needs, parents build a foundation of trust and security. This foundation fosters a strong parent-child bond and enables children to develop a sense of security and attachment.

In summary, CBT plays a crucial role in building strong bonds between parents and children. It enhances communication, promotes emotional regulation, challenges negative thoughts, develops problem-solving skills, and fosters trust and security. By implementing CBT principles and techniques, parents can create a nurturing and supportive environment that strengthens the parent-child relationship, promotes emotional well-being, and supports the healthy development of their children.

CHAPTER 2

FOUNDATIONS OF EFFECTIVE PARENTING

2.1 The Core Principles of CBT for Parents

The core principles of Cognitive Behavioral Therapy (CBT) for parents encompass fundamental concepts and approaches that guide the application of CBT techniques in parenting. These are some tactics you can employ:

1. **Recognizing and Restructuring Negative Thought Patterns:** CBT emphasizes the importance of identifying negative thought patterns and reframing them into more realistic and positive ones. Parents learn to recognize their negative thoughts and beliefs that may impact their parenting style and interactions with their children. By challenging and replacing these negative thoughts, parents can adopt more constructive and supportive thinking patterns that positively influence their behavior and the parent child relationship.

2. **Encouraging Positive Self-Talk for Parents and Children:** CBT emphasizes the role of self talk in influencing emotions and behaviors. Parents are encouraged to cultivate positive self talk, offering themselves compassion, understanding, and encouragement. Similarly, parents can help children develop positive self talk by teaching them to reframe negative thoughts into more empowering and optimistic ones. Positive self-talk enhances self-esteem, and resilience, and fosters a nurturing parent-child relationship.

3. Promoting Emotional Regulation and Resilience: Emotional regulation is a crucial aspect of parenting. CBT equips parents with strategies to recognize, understand, and manage their emotions effectively. By modeling healthy emotional regulation, parents teach their children valuable skills to identify and cope with their own emotions. This promotes emotional resilience, reduces conflicts, and fosters a more supportive parent-child relationship.

4. Enhancing Problem-Solving and DecisionMaking Skills: CBT emphasizes the development of problem-solving and decisionmaking skills for parents. Parents learn to break down complex problems into manageable steps, evaluate different solutions, and make informed decisions. By involving children in the problemsolving process and teaching them these skills, parents foster autonomy, and responsibility, and strengthen the parent-child bond through collaboration.

By integrating these core principles into their parenting approach, parents can enhance their understanding of themselves and their children, promote healthy communication, foster emotional well-being, and build a strong and positive parent-child relationship.

These principles form the foundation of CBT for parents and serve as guiding principles in navigating the challenges of parenting with a focus on growth, connection, and effective strategies.

2.2 Recognizing and Restructuring Negative Thought Patterns

Recognizing and restructuring negative thought patterns in children using Cognitive Behavioral Therapy (CBT) involves helping them identify and challenge unhelpful thoughts and replace them with more positive and realistic ones. These are some tactics you can employ:

1.   Create Awareness: Help your child become aware of their thoughts by encouraging them to pay attention to their internal dialogue.

Teach them to recognize negative self-talk or automatic negative thoughts that may arise in certain situations.

2. Identify Thinking Errors: Teach your child about common thinking errors or cognitive distortions, such as all-or-nothing thinking, overgeneralization, and personalization. Help them recognize when they engage in these thinking patterns and how they can impact their emotions and behaviors.

3. Challenge Negative Thoughts: Encourage your child to question the accuracy and validity of their negative thoughts. Ask them for evidence to support or contradict their negative beliefs. Help them understand that thoughts are not always facts and that alternative explanations or interpretations are possible.

4. Offer Alternative Perspectives: Assist your child in generating alternative, more positive and realistic thoughts that counter their negative beliefs. Help them find evidence that supports these alternative thoughts. Encourage them to consider different viewpoints and possibilities.

5.   Practice Positive Self-Talk: Teach your child the importance of positive self-talk and guide them in replacing negative statements with positive and affirming ones. Encourage them to use words of encouragement, self-compassion, and optimism when faced with challenges or setbacks.

6.   Reinforce Positive Experiences: Help your child focus on positive experiences, achievements, and strengths. Encourage them to reflect on their successes, however small they may be. By highlighting their positive qualities and accomplishments, you can reinforce positive self-perception and counteract negative thoughts.

7. Model Positive Thinking: Be a positive role model by demonstrating healthy thought patterns yourself. Share your own experiences of recognizing and challenging negative thoughts.

This can help normalize the process for your child and show them that it is a skill they can develop. Remember, practicing these strategies requires patience, consistency, and support. Be understanding and empathetic towards your child's struggles and guide them in a nurturing and non-judgmental manner. If needed, consider involving a qualified mental health professional who specializes in CBT to provide additional support and guidance in working with your child.

2.3 Encouraging Positive Self-Talk for Parents and Children

Cognitive Behavioral Therapy (CBT) plays a vital role in encouraging positive self-talk for both parents and children. Positive self-talk involves cultivating a positive and supportive internal dialogue, which can enhance self-esteem, resilience, and overall well-being. Here's how CBT promotes positive self-talk:

1.   **Increasing Self-Awareness:** CBT helps parents and children become aware of their inner thoughts and self-talk patterns. By recognizing negative or self-defeating thoughts, they can take the first step toward transforming them into more positive and supportive ones.

2.   **Challenging Negative Thoughts:** CBT teaches individuals to challenge and question negative thoughts. Parents and children learn to examine the evidence for and against these thoughts, identify cognitive distortions, and consider alternative interpretations. This process helps replace negative self-talk with more realistic and constructive thoughts.

3.   **Cognitive   Restructuring:**   Through cognitive restructuring techniques, CBT guides parents and children in reframing negative thoughts and replacing them with positive, affirming statements. They learn to identify and challenge self-limiting beliefs and replace them with empowering and encouraging thoughts. This practice builds self-confidence and fosters a positive mindset.

4.   Coping with Setbacks: CBT helps parents and children develop resilience and the ability to bounce back from setbacks. By reframing negative experiences as learning opportunities and using positive self-talk during challenging times, individuals can maintain a resilient mindset and foster perseverance.

5.   Reinforcing Positive Affirmations: CBT encourages the use of positive affirmations as a way to enhance positive self-talk. Parents and children can create and repeat personalized affirmations that focus on their strengths, accomplishments, and positive qualities. Regularly reinforcing these affirmations can improve self-esteem and self-belief.

6.   Modeling Positive Self-Talk: Parents serve as powerful role models for their children. By practicing positive self-talk themselves, parents demonstrate the importance and effectiveness of nurturing one's inner dialogue. Children observe and learn from their parents' examples, making positive self-talk a natural part of their thought processes.

7. **Celebrating Successes:** CBT emphasizes the recognition and celebration of successes, no matter how small. Parents and children learn to acknowledge and praise their achievements, reinforcing positive self-talk and fostering a sense of accomplishment.

By incorporating these CBT techniques into daily life, parents and children can cultivate a habit of positive self-talk. This promotes self compassion, resilience, and a more optimistic outlook, strengthening their overall well-being and supporting healthy parent-child relationships.

2.4 Promoting Emotional Regulation and Resilience

Cognitive Behavioral Therapy (CBT) plays a significant role in promoting emotional regulation and resilience for parenting. Here's how CBT can contribute to these areas:

1. **Understanding Emotions:** CBT helps parents gain a deeper understanding of their own emotions and the emotions of their children.

By recognizing and labeling emotions, parents can better identify their triggers and respond more thoughtfully and effectively. This understanding allows for greater emotional regulation and empathy in parenting interactions.

2. Identifying Negative Thought-Emotion Patterns: CBT teaches parents to identify the connection between negative thoughts and emotions. Parents learn to recognize unhelpful thinking patterns that contribute to emotional distress, such as catastrophizing or personalizing. By understanding how thoughts influence emotions, parents can intervene and reframe their thinking to promote healthier emotional responses.

3. Coping Strategies: CBT equips parents with a variety of coping strategies to manage and regulate their own emotions. These strategies may include relaxation techniques, mindfulness exercises, deep breathing, or engaging in enjoyable activities. By practicing these techniques, parents can model healthy emotional regulation to their children and guide them in managing their own emotions.

4. Teaching Children Emotional Regulation: CBT offers strategies for parents to teach their children emotional regulation skills. Parents can guide their children in identifying and expressing their emotions, understanding the physical sensations associated with emotions, and implementing coping techniques such as deep breathing or self-soothing activities. These skills empower children to manage their own emotions effectively and enhance their resilience.

5. Problem-Solving and Adaptive Thinking: CBT emphasizes problem-solving skills and adaptive thinking patterns. Parents can help their children develop these skills by encouraging them to evaluate situations objectively, consider different perspectives, and generate effective solutions. By engaging in problem-solving together, parents and children foster resilience and a sense of control in the face of challenges.

6.   Emotion Regulation Tools: CBT provides parents with specific tools to help regulate emotions within themselves and their children. These tools may include creating emotion regulation plans, implementing structured routines, using visual aids to express emotions, or utilizing calming techniques such as counting or visualization.

These tools assist parents in promoting emotional regulation and resilience in their parenting practices.

By incorporating CBT principles and techniques, parents can promote emotional regulation and resilience within themselves and their children. This not only enhances their well-being but also creates a supportive and emotionally balanced environment for the entire family.

2.5 Enhancing Problem-Solving and Decision-Making Skills

Enhancing problem-solving and decision-making skills as a parent is essential for effective parenting. Here are some methods to sharpen these abilities:

1.   Identify and Define the Problem: Identify the specific issue or challenge you're facing as a parent. Break it down into smaller, manageable parts to better understand its components.

2.   Generate Multiple Solutions: Encourage yourself to brainstorm multiple potential solutions to the problem. Don't assess them or judge them at this time. Simply focus on generating as many ideas as possible.

3.   Evaluate the Pros and Cons: Assess the advantages and disadvantages of each potential solution. Consider the potential outcomes, impact on all family members involved, and any potential risks or drawbacks associated with each option.

4.   Consider Values and Priorities: As a parent, have faith in your judgment and instincts. Consider how each solution aligns with these values and the long-term goals you have for your family

5. **Select the Best Solution:** Based on the evaluation and consideration of the pros and cons, choose the solution that appears to be the most beneficial and appropriate for the situation. Trust your judgment and intuition as a parent.

6. **Implement the Chosen Solution:** Put the selected solution into action. Develop a plan and follow through with the necessary steps to address the problem or make the decision.

7. **Reflect and Learn:** After implementing the solution, take time to reflect on the outcome. Evaluate how well it worked and if any adjustments are necessary. Learning from each experience will help you refine your problem-solving and decision-making skills over time.

8. **Involve Children in Problem-Solving:** Depending on their age and maturity, involve your children in problem-solving and decision-making processes. This helps them develop critical thinking skills, independence, and a sense of ownership over the outcomes.

9.   Seek Support and Guidance: Don't hesitate to seek support and guidance from trusted sources, such as other parents, support groups, or professionals.   They can provide insights, perspectives, and advice that may enhance your problem-solving and decision-making abilities.

10.   Practice Self-Care: Taking care of your own well-being is crucial for effective problem-solving and decision-making. When you're physically and emotionally balanced, you can approach challenges with a clear mind and better problem-solving abilities.

Remember that problem-solving and decision-making skills develop with practice and experience. Be patient with yourself and acknowledge that not every decision will be perfect. By continuously honing your skills, you'll become more confident and proficient in navigating the challenges of parenting.

CHAPTER 3

ESTABLISHING A SUPPORTIVE AND NURTURING ENVIRONMENT

3.1 Creating a Safe Space for Open Communication

Creating a safe space for open communication as a parent is vital for fostering trust, understanding, and healthy relationships with your children. Cognitive Behavioral Therapy (CBT) strategies can support this process. Here's how you can utilize CBT strategies to create a safe space for open communication:

1.   Active Listening: Practice active listening when your child communicates with you. Maintain eye contact, pay them your entire attention, and act genuinely interested in what they are saying. Reflect back what they've shared to ensure you understand their perspective accurately.

2.   Non-Judgmental Attitude: Adopt a non-judgmental and accepting attitude towards your child's thoughts, feelings, and experiences. Avoid criticizing or belittling their emotions or opinions. Create an environment where they feel safe expressing themselves without fear of judgment or punishment.

3.   Empathy and Validation: Show empathy and validate your child's emotions. Let them know that you understand and acknowledge their feelings, even if you may not agree with their perspective. Validating their emotions helps them feel heard and respected.

4.   Open and Honest Communication: Model open and honest communication with your child. Be transparent about your own thoughts, feelings, and experiences.

Encourage them to do the same by creating an environment where they feel comfortable sharing their thoughts and emotions without fear of negative consequences.

5. **Teach Effective Communication Skills:** Use CBT techniques to teach your child effective communication skills. This includes teaching them how to express their needs and emotions assertively, actively listening to others, and resolving conflicts through respectful dialogue.

6. **Encourage Problem-Solving:** Guide your child in problem-solving using CBT principles. Encourage them to think critically, explore different perspectives, and generate potential solutions. Help them evaluate the pros and cons of each option and support them in implementing their chosen solution.

7. **Manage Your Own Reactions:** Practice emotional regulation and manage your own reactions when your child communicates with you. Stay calm and composed, even when discussing sensitive or challenging topics.

Your own emotional regulation sets an example and creates a safe space for your child to express themselves freely.

8.   Provide Support and Validation: Offer support and validation to your child's thoughts and emotions. Help them develop coping strategies and problem-solving skills when they face difficulties. Let them know that you are there to support and guide them through challenges without judgment.

9.   Regular Check-Ins: Schedule regular check-ins with your child to discuss their thoughts, feelings, and any concerns they may have. Create a routine where they know they can approach you for open and honest conversations.

10.   Seek Professional Help if Needed: If you encounter challenges in creating a safe space for open communication, consider seeking guidance from a qualified mental health professional trained in CBT. They can offer you extra advice and assistance that is catered to your particular circumstance.

By implementing these CBT strategies, you can create an environment where open communication thrives, fostering trust, understanding, and strong parent-child relationships.

3.2 Fostering Empathy and Understanding

Fostering empathy and understanding as a parent is crucial for nurturing healthy relationships and emotional intelligence in your children. Cognitive Behavioral Therapy (CBT) strategies can support you in cultivating empathy and understanding.

Here's how you can utilize CBT strategies to foster empathy and understanding as a parent:

1. **Role Modeling:** Be a role model of empathy and understanding. Demonstrate empathy in your interactions with others, including your children. Show genuine concern for their feelings, perspectives, and experiences. By modeling empathy, you provide a powerful example for your children to follow.

2.   Perspective-Taking: Encourage your children to consider the perspectives of others. Teach them to put themselves in someone else's shoes and imagine how they might be feeling in a particular situation. This helps develop empathy and an understanding of different viewpoints.

3.   Active Listening: Practice active listening when your children express their thoughts and feelings. Give them your full attention, maintain eye contact, and show genuine interest. Reflect on what they've shared to demonstrate that you understand and validate their emotions.

4.   Emotional Recognition and Labeling: Help your children recognize and label their own emotions. Use CBT techniques to teach them about different emotions and how to identify them. By developing emotional intelligence, children can better understand and empathize with the emotions of others.

5.   Cognitive Restructuring: Teach your children to challenge negative assumptions or stereotypes they may have about others. Help them recognize cognitive biases and promote open-mindedness.

Encourage them to consider alternative explanations and challenge their own biases and prejudices.

6.   Perspective-Shifting Exercises: Engage in perspective-shifting exercises with your children. Explore different scenarios and discuss how different individuals might perceive and experience them. This helps broaden their understanding and empathy towards diverse perspectives.

7.   Encourage Empathy-Driven Actions: Encourage your children to translate their empathy into compassionate actions. Help them identify ways they can support and help others in need. Engage in community service or acts of kindness together as a family.

8.   Emotional Regulation Skills: Teach your children emotional regulation skills to manage their own emotions effectively. This enables them to approach situations with empathy and understanding, even in challenging circumstances.

9. **Teach Conflict Resolution:** Guide your children in resolving conflicts through open communication, active listening, and seeking mutually beneficial solutions. Teach them to consider the emotions and perspectives of all parties involved and to approach conflicts with empathy and understanding.

10. **Foster Respect for Diversity:** Promote respect for diversity in your family. Teach your children about different cultures, backgrounds, and perspectives. Encourage them to appreciate and celebrate diversity, fostering empathy and understanding towards others.

By integrating these CBT strategies into your parenting approach, you can foster empathy and understanding in your children. These skills lay the foundation for building compassionate and empathetic individuals who contribute positively to their relationships and communities.

3.3 Setting Realistic Expectations for Parenting and Growth

Setting realistic expectations for parenting and personal growth is essential for maintaining a balanced and healthy mindset. Cognitive Behavioral Therapy (CBT) strategies can help you establish realistic expectations and promote personal growth. Here's how you can utilize CBT strategies to set realistic expectations:

1. **Identify Cognitive Distortions:** Become aware of cognitive distortions, such as all-or nothing thinking, overgeneralization, or mental filtering, that may lead to unrealistic expectations. Recognize when these distortions influence your perception of parenting and personal growth.

2. **Challenge Unrealistic Thoughts:** Challenge and reframe unrealistic thoughts and beliefs. Examine the evidence for and against them, and consider more balanced and realistic perspectives. Replace self-defeating thoughts with more rational and constructive ones.

3. **Practice Self-Compassion:** Cultivate self compassion by treating yourself with kindness and understanding.

Recognize that parenting and personal growth are ongoing processes with ups and downs. Embrace imperfections and acknowledge that mistakes are opportunities for learning and growth.

4.   Focus on Progress, Not Perfection: Shift your focus from striving for perfection to recognizing and celebrating progress.
Break down large goals into smaller, achievable steps, and acknowledge the effort and growth you and your family are making along the way.

5.   Set Specific and Attainable Goals: Set specific and attainable goals for parenting and personal growth. Be realistic about what is feasible given your current circumstances and resources. Break goals into manageable tasks and track your progress to stay motivated.

6.   Practice Mindfulness: Engage in mindfulness practices to stay present and grounded in the current moment. Mindfulness helps you avoid getting caught up in unrealistic expectations or excessive worry about the future. It promotes acceptance of the present reality and fosters a sense of calm and clarity.

7.   Seek Social Support: Connect with other parents or support groups to gain perspective and share experiences. Surrounding yourself with a supportive community can help normalize challenges and provide valuable insights, reminding you that you're not alone in your journey.

8.   Reflect and Learn from Mistakes: Embrace mistakes and setbacks as opportunities for growth. Reflect on challenges or failures, identify lessons learned, and use them as stepping stones for personal growth and improved parenting strategies.

9.   Practice Self-Care: Prioritize self-care to maintain physical and emotional well-being. You can be the best version of yourself for your family if you take care of yourself. Remember that selfcare is not selfish but essential for effective parenting and personal growth.

10.   Celebrate Achievements: Celebrate both small and significant achievements along your parenting and personal growth journey.

11. Acknowledge and appreciate the progress you've made, reinforcing positive reinforcement and fostering a sense of accomplishment.

By incorporating these CBT strategies into your mindset and daily practices, you can set realistic expectations for parenting and personal growth. This enables you to navigate challenges with resilience, maintain a positive outlook, and cultivate a healthy and fulfilling family life.

3.4 Strengthening Parental Self-Care

Strengthening parental self-care is crucial for maintaining your well-being and effectively managing the demands of parenting. Cognitive Behavioral Therapy (CBT) strategies can support you in prioritizing self-care. Here's how you can utilize CBT strategies to strengthen parental selfcare:

1. **Recognize the Importance of Self-Care:** Understand that self-care is not selfish but essential for your overall well-being and ability to be a present and effective parent. Recognize that taking care of yourself allows you to better care for your children.

2. **Challenge Guilt and Negative Beliefs:** Challenge any guilt or negative beliefs that may hinder your self-care efforts. Replace thoughts like "I should always put my children's needs first" with more balanced and realistic beliefs that acknowledge the importance of self-care.

3. **Identify Self-Care Activities:** Identify activities that bring you joy, relaxation, and rejuvenation. This can include hobbies, exercise, meditation, reading, spending time with friends, or engaging in creative outlets. Choose activities that align with your interests and make you feel recharged.

4. **Schedule Self-Care Time:** Set aside dedicated time for self-care regularly. Consider making this pledge to yourself non-negotiable. Schedule it in your calendar and communicate your self-care needs with your family, setting boundaries and expectations.

5. **Practice Self-Compassion:** Practice self compassion by being kind and understanding towards yourself. Embrace imperfections and let go of self-judgment. Treat yourself with the same level of care and compassion you would offer to a loved one.

6. **Manage Time Effectively:** Use CBT techniques to manage your time effectively, ensuring you have dedicated moments for selfcare. Prioritize tasks, delegate responsibilities, and eliminate unnecessary time-wasting activities to create space for self-care activities.

7. **Challenge Negative Thought Patterns:** Identify negative thought patterns, such as self-critical or self-sacrificing thoughts, and challenge them using CBT techniques. Replace negative thoughts with positive affirmations that emphasize the importance of self-care and wellbeing.

8. **Practice Stress Management Techniques:** Learn and practice stress management techniques, such as deep breathing, mindfulness, or relaxation exercises. These techniques can help you manage stress effectively and find moments of calm amidst the demands of parenting.

9. **Seek Support:** Reach out for support from your partner, family members, or friends. Communicate your need for self-care and ask for assistance in managing parental responsibilities. Surround yourself with a support network that encourages and validates your self-care efforts.

10. **10. Monitor Self-Care Progress:** Regularly assess and monitor your self-care progress. Reflect on how you feel before and after engaging in self-care activities. Notice the positive impact they have on your well-being and parenting abilities, reinforcing the importance of self-care in your routine.

By integrating these CBT strategies into your parenting journey, you can strengthen parental self-care. Prioritizing your well-being not only benefits you but also enhances your ability to be a nurturing and present parent for your children. Remember, taking care of yourself is an investment in your family's overall happiness and health.

CHAPTER 4

EFFECTIVE COMMUNICATION TECHNIQUES

4.1 Active Listening and Validation

Active listening and validation are powerful techniques that can greatly enhance your communication with your child. Here's how you can apply them in your parenting:

1. **Give your full attention:** When your child wants to talk to you, put aside distractions such as phones or other tasks. Make eye contact and face them directly to show that you are fully engaged in the conversation.

2. **Listen without interrupting:** Allow your child to express themselves without interruption.

3. Avoid jumping in with your own thoughts or opinions. Instead, give them the space to share their thoughts, feelings, and experiences.

4. **Show nonverbal cues:** Use nonverbal cues such as nodding, smiling, and maintaining an open posture to convey that you are actively listening. These cues reassure your child that you are interested in what they have to say

5. **Reflect on their feelings:** Validate your child's emotions by acknowledging their feelings. You can say things like, "I can understand why you feel upset about that" or "It sounds like you're excited about your upcoming event." This shows empathy and lets them know that their emotions are valid.

6. **Paraphrase and summarize:** Repeat or summarize what your child has said to ensure that you've understood them correctly. This helps clarify any misinterpretations and shows that you value their perspective. Say something like, "So, what I'm hearing is that you're feeling left out because your friends didn't invite you to their gathering."

7.   Avoid judgment or criticism: While listening, refrain from passing judgment or criticizing your child's thoughts or feelings. Remember that active listening is about understanding and validating their perspective, even if you disagree.

8.   Use open-ended questions: Encourage your child to share more by asking open-ended questions. These questions cannot be answered with a simple "yes" or "no" and allow for more in-depth discussions. For example, ask, "How did that situation make you feel?" or "Can you tell me more about what happened?"

9.   Validate their experiences: Let your child know that their experiences matter and that you take them seriously. Avoid dismissing or trivializing their concerns. Even if you don't fully understand or agree with their viewpoint, respect their feelings and provide a supportive environment.

10. Respond with empathy: Respond to your child's disclosures or concerns with empathy and understanding. Show that you genuinely care about their well-being and that their feelings are important to you. Empathetic responses can include statements like, "That must have been tough for you" or "I can imagine how frustrating that situation must have been."

Remember, active listening and validation are ongoing practices. The more you incorporate them into your interactions with your child, the stronger your connection will become. These techniques not only foster open and honest communication but also contribute to your child's emotional well-being and sense of self-worth.

4.2 Assertive Communication and Setting Boundaries

Communicating assertively and setting boundaries as a parent is important for establishing a healthy and respectful relationship with your child.

Here are some strategies to help you communicate assertively and set boundaries effectively:

1. Be clear and specific: Clearly communicate your expectations, rules, and boundaries to your child. Use direct and specific language so there is no room for confusion or misinterpretation.

2. Use "I" statements: Express your needs and concerns using "I" statements instead of "you" statements. For example, say, "I feel upset when my things are taken without permission" rather than "You always take my things without asking. **3. State the behavior and its impact:** When addressing a specific behavior, describe it objectively and explain how it affects you or others. This helps your child understand the consequences of their actions. For instance, say, "When you leave your toys on the floor, I can trip and hurt myself."

4. Be firm and consistent: Stick to your boundaries and rules consistently. Avoid wavering or making exceptions, as it can confuse your child and undermine the importance of the boundary.

5.   Use a calm and respectful tone: Communicate your boundaries in a calm and composed manner. Avoid shouting or using aggressive language, as it can escalate conflicts and hinder effective communication.

6.   Explain the rationale: Help your child understand the reason behind the boundary or rule. Provide explanations that are ageappropriate and help them see the importance of respecting boundaries.

7.   Encourage dialogue: Create an open and safe space for your child to express their thoughts and concerns about the boundaries you've set. Listen to their perspective and engage in a constructive dialogue, allowing them to ask questions and seek clarification.

8.   Offer alternatives and compromises: If appropriate, provide alternatives or compromises that still respect the boundary while giving your child some autonomy or flexibility. This can help them feel more involved and empowered in the decision-making process.

9. Model healthy boundaries: Show your child how to set boundaries by demonstrating them in your own interactions and relationships. This helps them understand the importance of boundaries and how to communicate them effectively.

10. Reinforce positive behavior: Acknowledge and praise your child when they respect the established boundaries. Positive reinforcement encourages them to continue practicing respectful behavior.

Remember that setting boundaries is not about being controlling or rigid. It is about creating a safe and respectful environment that promotes healthy development and well-being for your child. By communicating assertively and setting boundaries effectively, you are teaching your child valuable skills for navigating relationships and respecting the boundaries of others.

4.3 Constructive Feedback and Conflict Resolution

Constructive feedback and conflict resolution are essential tools for effective parenting. When combined with Cognitive Behavioral Therapy (CBT) strategies, they can promote positive behavior change and strengthen parent-child relationships. Here's how you can incorporate these elements into your parenting:

1. Constructive Feedback:

- Focus on behavior: When providing feedback to your child, focus on specific behaviors rather than personal traits. For example, say, "I noticed that you completed your homework on time," instead of "You're such a responsible person."

- Be specific and descriptive: Clearly identify the behavior you're addressing and describe its impact. This helps your child understand the consequences of their actions and the desired change. A good example would be, "When you share your toys with your sister, it makes her feel happy and included."

-       Offer praise and encouragement: Reinforce positive behaviors with praise and encouragement. Let your child know that you appreciate their efforts and the positive changes they make. This reinforces their motivation and builds self-esteem.

2. Conflict Resolution:

-       Promote open communication: Encourage your child to express their thoughts and feelings during conflicts. Create a safe space where both of you can openly discuss the issue at hand. Practice active listening and validate their emotions to foster understanding.

-       Teach problem-solving skills: Help your child develop problem-solving skills by involving them in finding solutions. Encourage brainstorming and exploring different perspectives. Collaboratively work on finding a resolution that satisfies both parties.

-       Teach assertiveness: Teach your child to express their needs and concerns assertively, using "I" statements and respectful language.

This empowers them to communicate effectively and assert their boundaries without resorting to aggression or passive behavior.

- Encourage empathy and perspective-taking: Help your child understand the perspectives of others involved in the conflict. Encourage empathy by asking questions like, "How do you think your sibling feels about this situation?" This fosters comprehension and aids in the development of empathy in them.

- Model conflict resolution: Demonstrate healthy conflict resolution by managing your own conflicts in a constructive manner. Your child learns by observing your behaviour, so be a positive role model for them.

3. CBT Strategies:

- Cognitive Restructuring: Teach your child to identify and challenge negative or unhelpful thoughts that contribute to conflicts. Help them replace these thoughts with more realistic and positive ones, fostering healthier attitudes and behaviors.

-       Problem-Solving Techniques: Teach your child problem-solving strategies such as breaking down problems into smaller steps, considering alternative solutions, and evaluating the pros and cons of each option. This equips them with effective problem-solving skills that can be used in conflict resolution.

-       Emotional Regulation: Help your child recognize and manage their emotions during conflicts. Teach them relaxation techniques, deep breathing exercises, and positive coping skills to regulate their emotions and approach conflicts calmly and constructively.

By incorporating constructive feedback, conflict resolution skills, and CBT strategies into your parenting, you create an environment that supports growth, resilience, and healthy communication. These strategies help your child develop self-awareness, emotional intelligence, and effective problem-solving abilities, which are valuable life skills.

4.4 Building Trust and Strengthening Bonds through Communication

Building trust and strengthening bonds through communication is vital for healthy parent-child relationships. Here are a few techniques for doing this:

1. Create a Safe and Open Environment:
Foster an environment where your child feels safe to express themselves without fear of judgment or criticism. Encourage open and honest communication by actively listening, being supportive, and showing empathy.

2. **Be Reliable and Consistent:** Follow through on your commitments and promises to your child. Consistency in your actions and words helps build trust and reliability. This includes being consistent in your discipline, routines, and expectations.

3. **Practice Active Listening: Give** your child your full attention when they speak. Show genuine interest in what they have to say and provide them with your undivided attention. Reflect on what they say to show that you understand and value their perspective.

4. **Be Responsive and Available:** Make yourself available for your child when they need to talk or have questions. Respond to their messages, concerns, and needs on time. Show them that they can rely on you for support and guidance.

5. **Validate and Empathize:** Validate your child's emotions and experiences. Let them know that their feelings are understood and accepted, even if you may not agree with their actions. Show empathy by trying to understand their perspective and demonstrating that you genuinely care.

6. **Communicate Respectfully:** Model respectful communication by using polite language, avoiding derogatory or demeaning remarks, and treating your child with respect. Demonstrate to them the value of their thoughts and feelings.

7. **Share Quality Time:** Engage in activities and spend quality time together. This could involve participating in their interests, and hobbies, or simply having meaningful conversations. This shared time helps create bonds and strengthens the parent-child relationship.

8. **Be Transparent and Honest: Be** honest with your child in an age-appropriate manner. Avoid withholding information or lying as it undermines trust. If mistakes are made, acknowledge them, apologize, and work towards resolution.

9. **Encourage Independence and Autonomy:** Foster independence and decision-making skills in your child. Give them age-appropriate responsibilities and allow them to make choices. This shows that you trust their judgment and helps build their self-confidence.

10. **Celebrate Achievements:** Acknowledge and celebrate your child's accomplishments, both big and small. Recognize their efforts and praise them for their achievements. This positive reinforcement builds their self-esteem and reinforces the bond between them.

Remember, building trust and strengthening bonds takes time and consistent effort.

By incorporating these communication strategies into your parenting approach, you can create a supportive and nurturing environment that promotes a strong and trusting relationship with your child.

CHAPTER 5

BUILDING EMOTIONAL INTELLIGENCE IN CHILDREN

5.1 Understanding and Managing Emotions

Understanding and managing emotions as a parent is essential for creating a positive and nurturing environment for both yourself and your child. You can use the following tactics to aid you in this process:

1. Self-awareness: Start by developing self-awareness of your own emotions. Pay attention to your feelings, triggers, and patterns of emotional reactions.

2. Understand how your emotions may influence your parenting style and interactions with your child.

3. **Validate your emotions:** It's important to acknowledge and validate your own emotions. Understand that it's normal to experience a wide range of emotions as a parent, including frustration, stress, and even guilt. Recognize that these emotions are valid and don't judge yourself for feeling them.

4. **Reflect on your upbringing:** Reflect on how your upbringing and experiences with emotions may impact your current parenting style. Be mindful of any patterns or biases you may have inherited and consider how you can adjust your approach accordingly.

5. **Emotional regulation:** Practice techniques for managing your emotions effectively. This can include deep breathing exercises, mindfulness, physical activity, journaling, or seeking support from a therapist or support group. Learning to regulate your own emotions can positively influence your ability to respond to your child's emotions.

6.   Active listening and empathy: Develop strong listening skills and practice empathy towards your child's emotions. Pay attention to their non-verbal cues and try to understand their perspective. Validate their emotions by acknowledging and empathizing with their feelings, even if you don't agree with their behavior.

7.   Teach emotional intelligence: Help your child develop emotional intelligence by teaching them to recognize and express their own emotions. Encourage them to label their feelings and explore healthy ways to cope with them. Model healthy emotional expression and regulation.

8.   Create a safe space for emotions: Foster an environment where your child feels safe to express their emotions without judgment or punishment. Encourage open communication and let them know that it's okay to feel and express their emotions. Avoid dismissing or minimizing their feelings.

9. **Problem-solving and conflict resolution:**
Teach your child problem-solving skills and
healthy conflict resolution strategies. Help them
understand that conflicts and disagreements are
normal but can be resolved in respectful and
constructive ways. Guide them through problem-
solving processes and encourage compromise and
active listening.

10. **Seek support when needed:** Parenting can
be challenging, and it's important to seek support
when you need it. Reach out to friends, family, or
professionals who can offer guidance and
understanding. Join support groups or seek
therapy if necessary, to help you manage your
own emotions and navigate parenting challenges.
Remember, managing emotions is an ongoing
process. As you and your child learn and develop
together, use patience. By understanding and
managing your own emotions, you create a
foundation for supporting your child's emotional
well-being and developing a strong parent-child
relationship.

5.2 Teaching Emotional Regulation Skills

Teaching emotional regulation skills to your child is an important aspect of their overall emotional development. Here are some strategies to help you effectively teach and nurture these skills as a parent:

1. **Lead by Example**: Children learn a great deal from observing their parents. Model healthy emotional regulation by managing your own emotions positively and constructively. Demonstrate techniques like deep breathing, self-calming strategies, and positive coping mechanisms when you encounter challenging situations.

2. **Label Emotions:** Help your child develop emotional awareness by labeling and identifying different emotions. Use basic, age-appropriate language for expressing emotions. For example, say, "I can see that you're feeling frustrated right now. Would you like to talk about it?"

3. Create a Safe and Supportive Environment: Establish an environment where your child feels comfortable expressing their emotions without fear of judgment or punishment. Encourage open communication and assure them that it is okay to feel and express their emotions.

4. Teach Relaxation Techniques: Teach your child relaxation techniques to help them calm down when they are experiencing intense emotions. Breathing exercises, visualization, progressive muscle relaxation, or engaging in calming activities like drawing or listening to soft music can be helpful.

5. Provide Perspective-Taking Opportunities: Help your child develop empathy and understand others' perspectives. Encourage them to consider how their actions may impact others and discuss different viewpoints. This fosters emotional understanding and empathy, which contributes to emotional regulation.

6.   Teach Problem-Solving Skills: Help your child develop problem-solving skills to deal with emotional challenges. Teach them to identify the problem, brainstorm potential solutions, evaluate the pros and cons, and choose the most appropriate solution. Encourage them to reflect on the outcomes and adjust their approach if needed.

7.   Establish Healthy Coping Strategies: Encourage your child to engage in healthy coping strategies when they feel overwhelmed by emotions. This can include activities such as talking to a trusted adult, engaging in physical exercise, practicing a hobby, or writing in a journal. Aid them in locating constructive emotional outlets.

8.   Set Realistic Expectations: Understand that emotional regulation is a skill that develops over time. Set realistic expectations for your child and be patient with their progress. Offer support and guidance as they navigate their emotions.

9.   Encourage Positive Self-Talk: Teach your child to use positive self-talk to manage their emotions. Help them recognize negative or unhelpful thoughts and replace them with positive and supportive thoughts. Encourage them to reframe situations in a more positive light.

10.   Celebrate Progress: Recognize and celebrate your child's efforts and progress in managing their emotions. Praise their attempts to regulate their emotions effectively and provide encouragement along their journey.

Remember that teaching emotional regulation skills is an ongoing process. Be consistent, patient, and supportive in your approach. By nurturing your child's emotional development and providing them with the tools to regulate their emotions, you help them build resilience, improve self-control, and foster healthy relationships.

5.3 Encouraging Empathy and Compassion

Encouraging empathy and compassion in parenting helps children develop a deep understanding and care for others. Here are some strategies to foster empathy and compassion in your child:

1.   Model Empathy: Be a role model by consistently demonstrating empathy and compassion in your interactions with others. Show kindness, understanding, and consideration in your words and actions. Your child picks up knowledge by watching how you act.

2.   Teach Perspective-Taking: Help your child understand different perspectives by encouraging them to put themselves in others' shoes. Prompt them to consider how someone else might be feeling or what they might be experiencing. This helps cultivate empathy and an understanding of others' emotions and experiences.

3.   Practice Active Listening: Teach your child the importance of active listening. Encourage them to listen attentively when others are speaking and to ask questions to gain a deeper understanding of their thoughts and feelings. This demonstrates respect and empathy towards others.

4.   Encourage Emotional Expression: Create a safe and non-judgmental environment for your child to express their own emotions. When they share their feelings, validate and acknowledge them. This helps them develop self-awareness and empathy towards their own emotions and the emotions of others.

5.   Teach Kindness and Compassionate Acts: Guide your child to engage in acts of kindness and compassion towards others. Encourage them to be helpful, supportive, and considerate. Engage in volunteer work or community service together to provide first-hand experiences of helping others.

6.   Discuss Feelings and Emotions: Have open conversations about feelings and emotions with your child. Help them identify and label emotions, and discuss the impact emotions can have on individuals. This encourages empathy by fostering an understanding of the complexity of emotions.

7.   Read Empathy-Building Books: Choose books that promote empathy and compassion as part of their themes. Read these books together with your child and discuss the characters' feelings, motivations, and experiences. This helps develop empathy and encourages conversations about empathy and compassion.

8.   Practice Gratitude: Encourage your child to cultivate a sense of gratitude for the positive things in their life. Help them recognize and appreciate the kindness and compassion shown by others. Gratitude fosters empathy by promoting an awareness of the positive impact of others' actions.

9. Encourage Problem-Solving and Conflict Resolution: Teach your child skills for resolving conflicts peacefully and finding win-win solutions. Help them understand the importance of considering others' perspectives and needs when working towards a resolution. This cultivates empathy and understanding of others' viewpoints.

10. Foster Diversity and Inclusion: Expose your child to diverse cultures, backgrounds, and experiences. Encourage them to respect and appreciate differences. Teach them about fairness, equality, and the importance of treating everyone with kindness and compassion.

Remember to be patient and consistent in your efforts to encourage empathy and compassion in your child. Celebrate their acts of empathy and reinforce positive behavior. By nurturing these qualities, you are equipping your child with valuable skills that contribute to their emotional well-being and the creation of a kinder and more compassionate world.

5.4 Supporting Healthy Expression of Feelings

Supporting healthy expression of feelings as a parent is crucial for your child's emotional development. Here are some tips to assist you in this process:

1.   Create a Safe and Non-Judgmental Environment: Foster an environment where your child feels safe to express their feelings without fear of criticism or punishment. Assure them that it is normal and healthy to have a range of emotions and that their feelings are valid and important.

2.   Active Listening: When your child expresses their feelings, practice active listening. Give them your full attention, maintain eye contact, and show genuine interest in what they are saying. Reflect on their feelings to let them know you understand and validate their emotions.

3.   Avoid Dismissing or Minimizing Feelings: Resist the urge to dismiss or minimize your child's feelings, even if they seem trivial to you.

Remember that their experiences and emotions are unique to them, and it's essential to respect and acknowledge their emotions, regardless of their intensity or cause.

4. Use Open-Ended Questions: Encourage your child to elaborate on their feelings by using open-ended questions. Instead of asking, "Are you sad?", enquire, "Can you elaborate on what is saddening you?". This helps them explore their emotions and articulate their thoughts.

5. Teach Emotional Vocabulary: Help your child expand their emotional vocabulary by introducing and discussing different emotions. Encourage them to use specific words to describe their feelings, such as happy, sad, frustrated, excited, or worried. This enhances their ability to identify and express their emotions effectively.

6. Encourage Artistic Expression: Art, such as drawing, painting, or writing, can provide a creative outlet for your child to express their feelings. Encourage them to use art as a form of self-expression and create a safe space where they can freely express themselves through their artwork.

7.   Model Healthy Emotional Expression: Demonstrate healthy ways to express emotions by openly and properly sharing your feelings. Model techniques such as taking deep breaths, journaling, or talking about your emotions constructively. This shows your child that expressing emotions is a normal and healthy part of life.

8.   Teach Problem-Solving Skills: Guide your child in finding constructive solutions to manage their emotions. Encourage them to explore different coping strategies such as deep breathing, taking a break, talking to a trusted adult, or engaging in a favorite activity. Help them understand that there are various ways to handle and navigate their emotions.

9.   Validate and Empathize: Validate your child's feelings and let them know that it is okay to experience a wide range of emotions. Show empathy by acknowledging and understanding their emotions, even if you may not always agree with their behavior. This helps them feel heard, understood, and supported.

10.   Seek Professional Help if Needed: If you notice persistent or intense emotional difficulties in your child, consider seeking professional help from a therapist or counselor who specializes in working with children. They can provide additional guidance and support tailored to your child's specific needs.

Remember that supporting the healthy expression of feelings is an ongoing process. By creating a safe and accepting environment, actively listening, and validating your child's emotions, you promote their emotional well-being and help them develop healthy coping skills for a lifetime.

CHAPTER 6

POSITIVE PARENTING APPROACHES

6.1 Using Positive Reinforcement and Rewards

Using positive reinforcement and rewards in parenting can be an effective way to encourage desired behaviors and promote positive development in children. When combined with Cognitive Behavioral Therapy (CBT) strategies, it can provide a structured and supportive approach to parenting. Here are some steps you can follow:

1. Set clear goals and expectations: Define specific behaviors or skills you want to encourage in your child. Make sure the goals are realistic and age-appropriate.

2. Break goals into smaller steps: Divide larger goals into smaller, manageable tasks. This allows your child to experience success more frequently and reinforces their progress.

3. Create a reward system: Establish a system where your child earns rewards or privileges for meeting their goals or demonstrating desired behaviors. Make sure the rewards are meaningful to your child and match their interests.

4. Discuss the system with your child: Explain the reward system clearly to your child, emphasizing the positive behaviors you want to see. Ensure they understand what is expected of them and what rewards they can earn.

5. Reinforce positive behaviors: Whenever your child exhibits the desired behavior, provide immediate positive reinforcement.

This can include verbal praise, a hug, a high-five, or any other positive gesture that acknowledges their effort.

6.   Use tangible rewards: In addition to verbal praise, you can also offer tangible rewards as incentives. These can include small treats, extra playtime, stickers, or special privileges. Make sure the rewards are consistent and proportionate to the effort put forth.

7.   Track progress: Keep a record of your child's progress and provide feedback regularly. This helps them see their accomplishments and stay motivated to continue their positive behaviors.

8.   Gradually fade the rewards: As your child becomes more proficient in the desired behavior, gradually reduce the frequency or magnitude of the rewards. This encourages intrinsic motivation and helps them internalize the desired behaviors.

9.   Be consistent and predictable: Consistency is key in reinforcing positive behaviors. Make sure the rules and rewards are consistently applied across different situations and caregivers.

10. Encourage self-monitoring: Teach your child to self-assess and monitor their behavior. Help them recognize their progress and reward themselves for meeting their goals.

11. Address setbacks positively: If your child struggles or exhibits undesired behaviors, avoid punishment or criticism. Instead, focus on problem-solving and finding strategies to overcome challenges together.

Remember, positive reinforcement and rewards should be used in conjunction with other parenting strategies, such as clear communication, setting boundaries, and providing emotional support. CBT techniques can help you and your child identify and challenge unhelpful thoughts or behaviors that may interfere with the reinforcement process.

6.2 Implementing Effective Discipline Strategies

Implementing effective discipline strategies is an essential aspect of parenting. Here are some strategies you can use to promote positive behavior and teach your child important life skills:

1.   Set clear and consistent rules: Establish ageappropriate rules that are easy to understand and enforce. Make sure the rules are consistent across different situations and caregivers.

2.   Explain the reasons behind the rules: Help your child understand why certain behaviors are expected and why certain rules are in place. This promotes their understanding and cooperation.

3.   Use positive reinforcement: Acknowledge and reward your child's good behavior. Praise and encourage them when they follow the rules or exhibit positive traits. This reinforces their positive actions and motivates them to continue behaving well.

4.   Establish logical consequences: When a child breaks a rule, implement logical consequences that are related to the behavior. For example, if a child refuses to clean up their toys, a consequence could be temporarily losing access to a favorite toy until they comply.

5.   Time-out technique: If your child's behavior is inappropriate or dangerous, you can use a timeout technique. Designate a specific area where your child can take a short break to calm down and reflect on their behavior. The duration of the time-out should be brief and age-appropriate.

6.   Set expectations in advance: Clearly communicate your expectations before entering a situation where misbehavior is likely. For example, before going to a restaurant, discuss appropriate behavior and the consequences of not following the rules.

7.   Be a positive role model: Children learn a great deal from observing their parents.

8.   Model the behavior you expect from them and demonstrate self-control, empathy, and problem-solving skills.

9.   Use redirection and distraction: If your child is engaged in undesired behavior, redirect their attention to a more appropriate activity or topic. Distraction can be effective in preventing conflict or addressing unwanted behaviors.

10.   Maintain open communication: Encourage your child to express their feelings and thoughts. Create a safe space where they can discuss their concerns, fears, or frustrations. This helps them develop emotional intelligence and problem-solving skills.

11.   Teach problem-solving skills: Guide your child in finding constructive solutions to conflicts or challenges. Help them brainstorm alternatives and consider the consequences of their actions.

12.   Provide natural consequences: Sometimes, allowing your child to experience the natural consequences of their actions can be an effective teaching tool. For instance, if they refuse to wear a jacket, they may feel cold and learn the importance of dressing appropriately.

13.　　Stay calm and composed: It's crucial to remain calm and composed when addressing challenging behavior. Take a deep breath, use a firm but gentle tone, and avoid engaging in power struggles or becoming overly emotional.

Remember, effective discipline focuses on teaching and guiding your child rather than simply punishing them. It's important to balance discipline with love, understanding, and open communication to foster a healthy and positive parent-child relationship.

6.3 Promoting Independence and Responsibility

Promoting independence and responsibility in children is an important aspect of their development. Cognitive Behavioral Therapy (CBT) strategies can be effective in achieving this goal. Here are some CBT-based strategies you can use as a parent to promote independence and responsibility:

1.   Set clear expectations and goals: Clearly define your expectations and goals for your child's behavior, responsibilities, and independence. Make sure these expectations are age-appropriate and realistic.

2.   Break tasks into manageable steps: Help your child develop a sense of competence and independence by breaking tasks into smaller, manageable steps. This makes it easier for them to learn and complete tasks on their own.

3. Teach problem-solving skills: CBT emphasizes problem-solving techniques. Teach your child how to identify problems, generate possible solutions, evaluate the pros and cons, and make decisions. Encourage them to think critically and find solutions to challenges they encounter.

4. Encourage self-reflection: Help your child develop self-awareness and self-reflection skills. Encourage them to think about their actions, emotions, and thoughts. Ask open-ended questions to help them explore their experiences and learn from them.

5. Use positive reinforcement: Reinforce and praise your child's efforts and achievements when they demonstrate independence and responsibility. Positive reinforcement strengthens desired behaviors and encourages them to continue taking responsibility for their actions.

6.   Foster a growth mindset: Teach your child about the concept of a growth mindset, which emphasizes the belief that abilities and intelligence can be developed through effort and practice. Encourage them to embrace challenges, persevere through setbacks, and view mistakes as learning opportunities.

7.   Provide opportunities for decision-making: Give your child opportunities to make age appropriate decisions. Start with small choices and gradually increase the complexity of the decisions they make. This helps them develop decision-making skills and a sense of responsibility.

8.   Encourage problem-focused thinking: Help your child focus on problem-solving rather than dwelling on negative thoughts or blaming others. Teach them to identify the problem, consider different solutions, and take proactive steps to address the issue.

9.   Model independence and responsibility: Be a role model for your child by demonstrating independence and responsibility in your actions. Show them how you handle challenges, make decisions, and take responsibility for your choices.

10.   Provide guidance and support: While encouraging independence, it's important to offer guidance and support. Be available to answer questions, provide assistance, and offer encouragement when needed. Gradually decrease the level of support as your child becomes more capable.

Remember, promoting independence and responsibility is a gradual process. It requires patience, consistency, and a supportive environment. CBT strategies can help foster these qualities in your child, but it's important to adapt them to your child's individual needs and developmental stage.

6.4 Nurturing Self-Esteem and Positive Self-Image

Nurturing self-esteem and a positive self-image in children is crucial for their emotional well-being. Here are some CBT-based strategies you can use as a parent to foster self-esteem and a positive self-image:

1. Encourage positive self-talk: Teach your child to recognize and challenge negative self-talk by replacing it with positive and realistic thoughts. Help them identify and reframe negative statements or self-criticisms into more positive and supportive statements.

2. Focus on strengths and achievements: Help your child identify and celebrate their strengths, talents, and achievements. Encourage them to recognize their abilities and the progress they make in various areas of their life. Acknowledge their efforts and highlight their successes.

3.   Foster realistic and balanced thinking: Teach your child to evaluate situations and themselves in a realistic and balanced manner. Help them challenge all-or-nothing thinking or overly negative self-evaluations. Encourage them to consider alternative perspectives and evidence that support a more balanced view.

4.   Promote self-compassion: Help your child develop self-compassion by encouraging them to treat themselves with kindness and understanding. Teach them to be gentle with themselves when facing challenges or setbacks, and to recognize that mistakes are a natural part of learning and growth.

5.   Encourage self-care: Teach your child the importance of taking care of their physical and emotional well-being. Encourage healthy habits such as regular exercise, proper nutrition, sufficient sleep, and engaging in activities they enjoy. Emphasize the connection between selfcare and self-esteem.

6. Provide a supportive and validating environment: Create an environment where your child feels safe, supported, and validated. Listen to their thoughts and feelings without judgment, and offer empathy and understanding. Validate their experiences and emotions, even if you may not agree with their perspective.

7. Foster a growth mindset: Help your child develop a growth mindset, which focuses on the belief that abilities can be developed through effort and practice. Encourage them to embrace challenges, persevere through setbacks, and view mistakes as opportunities for learning and growth.

8. Avoid excessive criticism or comparisons: Be mindful of the language you use when providing feedback or addressing mistakes. Avoid excessive criticism, harsh judgments, or comparisons to others. Instead, provide constructive feedback and focus on the process and effort rather than solely on outcomes.

9.   Encourage goal-setting and problem-solving: Help your child set realistic goals and develop problem-solving skills. Break down larger goals into smaller, achievable steps, and provide guidance and support as they work towards their objectives. This fosters a sense of competence and accomplishment.

10.   Model positive self-esteem and self-image: Be a positive role model by demonstrating healthy self-esteem and a positive self-image. Practice self-care, engage in positive self-talk, and embrace challenges and personal growth. Your child learns a lot from observing your behavior.

Remember that building self-esteem and a positive self-image is an ongoing process. Be patient and supportive, and adjust these strategies to fit your child's unique needs and developmental stage.

CHAPTER 7

Tools and Resources for Parental Growth

Practical Exercises and Activities for Parent-Child Bonding

Title: Parent-Child Bonding Worksheet for CBT for Parenting

Instructions: This worksheet contains practical exercises and activities to enhance parent-child bonding while incorporating Cognitive Behavioral Therapy (CBT) techniques. Complete each exercise with your child and discuss the experience afterwards.

Remember to be patient, compassionate, and non-judgmental towards yourself and your child.

Exercise 1: Mindful Listening

Objective: To practice active listening and improve communication skills.

Instructions:
1.   Find a quiet and comfortable place to sit with your child.
2.   Ask your child to share something they are interested in or passionate about.
3.   Listen attentively to what they are saying without interrupting or judging.
4.   After they finish, repeat back to them what you heard to ensure understanding.
5.   Switch roles and have your child listen to you share something you are interested in.

Discussion:
-     How did it feel to actively listen without interrupting or judging?
-     Did you feel understood when the other person repeated back what they heard?
-     How can we incorporate mindful listening into our daily interactions?

Exercise 2: Positive Self-Talk

Objective: To promote positive self-talk and selfesteem.

Instructions:

1.   Have your child write down three positive affirmations about themselves (e.g., "I am kind," "I am smart," "I am brave").

2.   Encourage them to say these affirmations out loud every morning and before bed.

3.   Help them come up with additional affirmations if needed.

4.   Model positive self-talk by sharing your affirmations with your child.

Discussion:

-       How did it feel to say positive affirmations about yourself?

-       Did you notice any changes in how you felt about yourself?

-       How can we continue to practice positive selftalk together?

Exercise 3: Gratitude Journaling

Objective: To cultivate gratitude and appreciation for the good things in life.

Instructions:
1. Have your child write down three things they are grateful for each day.
2. Encourage them to be specific and detailed (e.g., "I am grateful for my mom who always listens to me," "I am grateful for my cozy bed").
3. Share your gratitude list with your child.
4. Set aside time each week to read through past entries and reflect on the good things in life.

Discussion:
- How did it feel to focus on the positive things in life?
- Did you notice any changes in your mood or outlook?
- How can we continue to cultivate gratitude and appreciation together?

Exercise 4: Problem-Solving

Objective: To practice problem-solving skills and improve decision-making.

Instructions:

1. Choose a problem or challenge that you and your child are facing.
2. Brainstorm possible solutions together.
3. Evaluate each solution by considering the pros and cons.
4. Choose the best solution and create a plan of action.
5. Follow through with the plan and evaluate the outcome.

Discussion:

-      How did it feel to work together to solve a problem?

-      Did you learn anything new about each other during this exercise?

-      How can we continue to practice problemsolving skills together?

Parent-child bonding is essential for building strong relationships and promoting healthy development. Incorporating CBT techniques can enhance this bond by promoting positive communication, self-esteem, gratitude, and problem-solving skills. Remember to practice these exercises regularly and have fun!

7.1 Mindfulness Practices for Parents and Children

Mindfulness practices can be beneficial for both parents and children, promoting a sense of presence, emotional regulation, and overall wellbeing. Here are different mindfulness practices that parents and children can engage in:

1. Breathing Exercises:
- Belly Breathing: Sit comfortably and place a hand on the belly. Take slow, deep breaths, feeling the belly rise and fall with each inhale and exhale. Focus attention on the breath, letting go of distractions.

-      **Breathing:** Inhale through the nose for a count of 4, hold the breath for a count of 7, and exhale slowly through the mouth for a count of 8. Repeat several times.

2. Body Scan:

- Guide your child to lie down or sit comfortably. Starting from the top of the head, slowly guide their attention through each part of the body, noticing any sensations or tension. Encourage them to relax and let go of any tension they find.

3. Mindful Eating:

- Choose a snack or meal to eat mindfully. Encourage your child to engage all their senses in the experience, paying attention to the taste, texture, and smell of the food. Encourage them to eat slowly and savor each bite.

4. Sensory Awareness:

- Take a mindful walk with your child. Encourage them to notice the sounds, smells, and sights around them. Draw their attention to the feeling of their feet on the ground or the sensation of the wind on their skin.

5. Gratitude Practice:

- Each day, invite your child to identify three things they are grateful for. Encourage them to explore both big and small moments of gratitude. Model this practice by sharing your gratitude as well.

6. Loving-Kindness Meditation:

- Guide your child to repeat phrases of wellwishing towards themselves and others. For example, "May I be happy, may I be safe, may I be healthy. May [friend/family member] be happy, may [friend/family member] be safe, may [friend/family member] be healthy."

7. Mindful Movement:

- Engage in activities such as yoga or stretching exercises with your child. Encourage them to pay attention to their body, breath, and sensations during the movements. Emphasize the importance of being present and listening to their body.

8. Mindful Listening:

- Sit in a quiet space and close your eyes. Ask your child to listen carefully to all the sounds they can hear. After a few minutes, discuss and share what each of you noticed, without judgment or analysis.

9. Mindful Communication:

- Practice active listening with your child. Encourage them to express their thoughts and feelings openly while you provide your full attention. Reflect on what you hear to ensure understanding and connection. Remember to adapt these practices to your child's age and developmental level. Start with shorter sessions and gradually increase the duration as they become more comfortable with mindfulness practices. Regularly engage in these activities to cultivate a mindfulness habit and strengthen the parent-child bond.

7.2 Collaborative Problem-Solving Activities

Collaborative problem-solving activities can help parents and children work together to find solutions, improve communication, and strengthen their relationships. Here are some practical exercises for collaborative problem-solving:

1. Create an Invention:

Encourage your child's creativity by engaging in an invention activity. Discuss a common problem or challenge, such as organizing toys or managing time. Brainstorm ideas together and design an invention that could solve the problem. Encourage your child to draw or build prototype of their invention.

2. Plan a Family Outing:

Involve your child in planning a family outing or activity. Discuss different options and gather everyone's preferences. Together, research and evaluate the feasibility of each option.

Consider factors like cost, time, and accessibility. Collaboratively make a decision and create an itinerary for the outing.

3. Room Makeover:

Allow your child to take part in redecorating or organizing their room. Start by discussing their goals and preferences for the space. Brainstorm ideas together and plan the layout, colors, and decorations. Set a budget and involve your child in purchasing or making the necessary items. Work together to implement the changes.

4. Solving a Conflict:

Choose a common conflict scenario, such as sharing toys or resolving a disagreement. Act out the conflict with your child, taking turns playing different roles. Encourage open communication, active listening, and empathy. Together, brainstorm possible solutions and discuss the pros and cons of each option. Collaboratively choose the best solution and role-play the resolution.

5. Design a Chore System:

Involve your child in designing a chore system for the family. Start by discussing the household responsibilities and the importance of each task. Brainstorm different ways to divide and rotate the chores fairly. Create a visual chore chart together and discuss expectations and rewards. Regularly review and adjust the system based on feedback.

6. Meal Planning and Preparation:

Engage your child in meal planning and preparation activities. Collaboratively decide on a meal or menu for the week. Make a grocery list together and involve your child in shopping for the ingredients. During meal preparation, assign age-appropriate tasks and work together as a team. Encourage creativity and exploration in the kitchen.

7. Family Problem-Solving Game:

Create a problem-solving game where you and your child take turns presenting hypothetical problems or challenges. Discuss possible solutions and evaluate the outcomes.

Encourage your child to think critically and provide reasoning for their suggestions. This activity promotes collaborative thinking and decision-making skills.

8. Building a Model or Puzzle:

Select a complex model or puzzle that requires collaboration. Work together to read the instructions, divide tasks, and assemble the pieces. Encourage active communication, problem-solving, and patience throughout the process. Celebrate your joint accomplishment upon completion.

Remember, the key to collaborative problem-solving is actively involving your child in the decision-making process and valuing their input. These activities provide opportunities for teamwork, communication, critical thinking, and creativity while strengthening the parent-child bond.

7.3 Creative Expression and Art Therapy Techniques

Creative expression and art therapy techniques can be valuable tools for parenting, as they allow for emotional exploration, self-expression, and communication. When combined with Cognitive Behavioral Therapy (CBT) strategies, they can provide a holistic approach to support your child's emotional well-being. Here are some techniques that integrate creative expression and CBT principles:

1. Emotion Collage:

Encourage your child to create a collage using images, colors, and words that represent their emotions. Start by discussing different emotions and their corresponding physical sensations. Then, provide magazines, colored paper, markers, and glue for them to select and assemble their collage.

Afterwards, explore the emotions depicted and discuss coping strategies for each emotion.

2. Feelings Journal:

Invite your child to keep a feelings journal where they can freely express their emotions through writing, drawing, or a combination of both. Encourage them to write about their experiences, thoughts, and associated emotions. Encourage reflection on positive aspects and help them challenge any negative or distorted thoughts that may arise.

3. Mindful Art:

Guide your child through a mindful art session, focusing on the present moment and the sensory experience of creating art. Provide various art materials such as paints, markers, or clay. Encourage them to explore their emotions through colors, shapes, and textures. Discuss their artwork afterwards, exploring any emotions or insights that emerged during the process.

4. Narrative Drawing:

Invite your child to create a narrative drawing that tells a story or represents a personal experience.

Encourage them to incorporate details and symbols that convey their thoughts and feelings.

After completing the drawing, discuss the story behind it and explore any underlying emotions or thoughts.

5. Thought-Bubble Drawing:

Ask your child to draw a large thought bubble on a piece of paper. Inside the bubble, have them write or draw any negative thoughts or self-criticisms they may have. Encourage them to identify and challenge these thoughts by creating positive counter-thoughts outside the bubble. This exercise helps develop cognitive flexibility and challenges negative thinking patterns.

6. Collaborative Art:

Engage in a collaborative art activity with your child. Create a shared canvas or collage where both of you can contribute your artistic expressions. Use the artwork as a starting point for open conversations about feelings, thoughts, and experiences. This activity promotes bonding, empathy, and mutual understanding.

7. Feelings Wheel:

Create a "feelings wheel" together with your child. Draw a large circle and divide it into sections, each representing a different emotion. Ask your child to color each section based on how frequently they experience that emotion. Discuss the different emotions, their triggers, and healthy coping strategies for managing them.

8. Guided Imagery Art:

Guide your child through a visualization exercise where they imagine a peaceful or happy place. Afterwards, provide art materials and encourage them to create a visual representation of their imagined place. Discuss the emotions evoked by the artwork and explore ways to bring elements of that place into their daily lives.

Remember, the focus of these techniques is on self-expression, exploration, and fostering emotional well-being. Adapt them to your child's age and interests, and create a safe and non-judgmental environment that encourages open communication.

7.4 Strengthening the Parent-Child Relationship through Play

Playing with your child is a wonderful way to strengthen the parent-child relationship. Play allows for bonding, communication, and shared experiences. Here are some strategies to help you strengthen your relationship through play:

1.   Be fully present: When engaging in play with your child, make a conscious effort to be fully present and attentive. Put away distractions such as phones or work-related thoughts. Focus on enjoying the moment and creating a meaningful connection with your child.

2.   Follow their lead: Allow your child to take the lead in a play and follow their interests. Let them choose the activities and games they want to engage in. By doing so, you show respect for their autonomy and build trust in the relationship.

3. Active listening and empathy: During play, actively listen to your child's thoughts, ideas, and stories. Show genuine interest in their play narratives and emotions. Practice empathy by validating their experiences and reflecting their feelings to them.

4. Play their way: Enter your child's world of play and participate in their imaginative play scenarios. Actively engage in their play themes and characters. Use your imagination to create new possibilities and extend your play ideas. This fosters a sense of shared enjoyment and connection.

5. Incorporate cooperative play: Introduce games or activities that require cooperation and teamwork. Encourage your child to work together with you towards a common goal. This promotes collaboration, and problem-solving, and strengthens the bond between you.

6. Play outdoors: Spend time playing outdoors with your child. Go for walks, visit the park, or engage in physical activities together.

Outdoor play not only provides opportunities for fun and exploration but also enhances the parentchild bond through shared experiences in nature.

7.   Incorporate laughter and silliness: Find moments to be playful, silly, and lighthearted with your child. Engage in activities that elicit laughter and joy. Share jokes, tickle fights, or engage in physical play that allows for laughter and a sense of shared amusement.

8.   Play board games or puzzles: Engage in board games or puzzles that require turn-taking, strategy, and problem-solving. This type of play promotes communication, patience, and healthy competition in a fun and interactive way.

9.   Create special play rituals: Establish special play rituals that are unique to you and your child. It could be a weekly game night, a special activity on weekends, or a designated time for imaginative play. These rituals create anticipation, excitement, and a sense of shared connection.

10.   Reflect on play experiences: After play sessions, take time to reflect on the experience with your child. Discuss what you enjoyed, what you learned, and any feelings that arose. This reflection deepens the connection and helps build a sense of emotional intimacy.

Remember, the primary goal of playing with your child is to create a positive and nurturing environment for them to feel loved, valued and understood. Adapt the play activities to their age, interests, and developmental level. Enjoy the process of play and cherish the moments of connection with your child.

CHAPTER 8

Overcoming Common Parenting Challenges

8.1 Managing Behavioral Issues and Tantrums

Managing behavioral issues and tantrums can be challenging for parents. Here are some strategies to help you successfully manage these situations: 1. Stay calm and composed: It's important to stay calm and composed when dealing with behavioral issues or tantrums. Take a deep breath and remind yourself that your response sets the tone for the interaction. Responding with patience and composure helps de-escalate the situation.

2. Model and encourage emotional regulation: Teach your child healthy ways to express their emotions. Help them identify and label their feelings. Encourage them to use words to express themselves instead of resorting to tantrums. Model self-control and emotional regulation yourself, showing them how to manage frustrations and disappointments.

3. Set clear and consistent boundaries: Establish clear and consistent boundaries and rules for behavior. Communicate these expectations to your child positively and firmly. Be consistent in enforcing the consequences of their actions when they cross the boundaries.

4. Use positive reinforcement: Catch your child exhibiting positive behaviors and provide specific praise and positive reinforcement. This encourages them to repeat those behaviors. Recognize and reward their efforts in managing their emotions and behaving appropriately.

5. Utilize redirection: When you sense a tantrum or negative behavior building, redirect your child's attention to a more positive and engaging activity. Distracting them with something they enjoy or finding an alternative focus can help diffuse the situation.

6. Provide choices: Give your child age-appropriate choices within the boundaries you've set. This gives them a sense of autonomy and control. For example, offer them options for activities, clothing, or snacks, allowing them to feel a sense of ownership and responsibility.

7. Practice active listening: During moments of frustration, actively listen to your child. Give them space to express their feelings and thoughts. Show empathy and validate their emotions, even if you may not agree with their behavior. Understanding their perspective helps create a sense of trust and open communication.

8. Use logical consequences: When addressing behavioral issues, implement logical consequences that are related to misbehavior. For example, if a child refuses to clean up their toys, temporarily remove a preferred toy until they complete the task. Ensure that the consequences are age-appropriate and not excessively punitive.

9. Teach problem-solving skills: Help your child develop problem-solving skills by involving them in finding solutions to conflicts or challenges. Encourage them to think through the situation, generate possible solutions, and discuss the consequences of each option. This empowers them to make better choices in the future.

10. Seek support when needed: If you find it challenging to manage behavioral issues or tantrums, seek support from professionals such as pediatricians, therapists, or parenting classes. They can provide guidance, strategies, and additional resources tailored to your child's specific needs.

Remember, managing behavioral issues and tantrums requires patience, consistency, and understanding. Each child is unique, so it's important to find the strategies that work best for your child and your family dynamics.

8.2 Addressing Anxiety and Stress in Children

Addressing anxiety and stress in children requires a supportive and understanding approach. Here are some strategies to help you as a parent:

1.   Create a safe and nurturing environment: Foster a safe and nurturing environment at home where your child feels comfortable expressing their feelings and concerns. Ensure they have a sense of security and stability.

2.   Validate their emotions: Acknowledge and validate your child's feelings of anxiety and stress. Let them know that it's okay to feel anxious or stressed and that their emotions are valid. Avoid dismissing or minimizing their concerns.

3. Open communication: Encourage open and honest communication with your child. Create opportunities for them to talk about their worries

and fears. Listen attentively without judgment and show empathy and understanding.

4.   Teach relaxation techniques: Teach your child simple relaxation techniques such as deep breathing exercises, progressive muscle relaxation, or guided imagery. Practice these techniques together, particularly during moments of stress or anxiety.

5.   Help them identify triggers: Work with your child to identify the specific triggers that contribute to their anxiety or stress. By understanding their triggers, you can help them develop strategies to cope with those situations more effectively.

6.   Break tasks into manageable steps: Assist your child in breaking down tasks or challenges into smaller, more manageable steps. This helps prevent overwhelm and allows them to approach tasks in a more gradual and less anxietyprovoking manner.

7.   Encourage a healthy lifestyle: Promote a healthy lifestyle for your child, including regular exercise, nutritious meals, and sufficient sleep.

Physical well-being can have a positive impact on their mental and emotional well-being, reducing anxiety and stress.

8. Foster a routine: Establish a predictable routine for your child. Consistency and structure provide a sense of stability and security, which can help alleviate anxiety and stress. Ensure that the routine includes dedicated time for relaxation and enjoyable activities.

9. Encourage problem-solving skills: Help your child develop problem-solving skills to manage their anxiety and stress. Teach them to identify the problem, brainstorm possible solutions, and evaluate the pros and cons of each option. Encourage them to take small steps toward resolving the issue.

10. Seek professional help if needed: If your child's anxiety or stress significantly impacts their daily functioning or if you're concerned about their well-being, consider seeking professional help. A mental health professional can provide guidance, support, and appropriate interventions tailored to your child's needs.

Remember, addressing anxiety and stress in children is an ongoing process. Be patient and supportive, and recognize that each child may respond differently. Tailor your approach to your child's individual needs and seek professional help when necessary.

8.3 Dealing with Academic Pressure and Performance Anxiety

Dealing with academic pressure and performance anxiety in children requires a supportive and balanced approach. Cognitive Behavioral Therapy (CBT) strategies can help manage these challenges. Here are some strategies you can use as a parent:

1. Recognize and reframe negative thoughts: Help your child identify negative thoughts or beliefs that contribute to their academic pressure or performance anxiety. Teach them to challenge and reframe these thoughts with more realistic and positive ones.

2.   Encourage them to focus on their efforts, progress, and personal growth rather than solely on outcomes.

3.   Set realistic expectations: Foster a realistic and balanced approach to academic expectations. Encourage your child to strive for personal improvement and excellence rather than perfection. Help them set achievable goals based on their abilities and strengths.

4.   Promote a growth mindset: Teach your child about the concept of a growth mindset, which emphasizes the belief that abilities and intelligence can be developed through effort and practice. Encourage them to view challenges as opportunities for learning and growth rather than as threats to their self-worth.

5.   Break tasks into smaller steps: Help your child break down academic tasks into smaller, more manageable steps. Guide them in creating a study plan or schedule that allows for regular breaks and avoids last-minute cramming. Breaking tasks down can reduce overwhelm and increase their sense of control.

6.   Teach effective study skills: Help your child develop effective study skills, such as time management, organization, and active learning strategies. Guide them in finding study methods that work best for their learning style and preferences. This can increase their confidence and preparedness.

7.   Encourage self-care and stress management: Teach your child the importance of self-care and stress management techniques. Encourage them to engage in activities they enjoy, get regular exercise, practice relaxation techniques, and maintain a balanced lifestyle. These practices can help reduce anxiety and promote overall wellbeing.

8.   Foster a supportive environment: Create a supportive environment at home where mistakes and setbacks are seen as learning opportunities. Encourage open communication about their academic concerns and provide emotional support. Celebrate their efforts and progress, rather than solely focusing on grades or rankings.

9. Encourage self-compassion: Help your child develop self-compassion by teaching them to be kind and understanding toward themselves. Encourage them to embrace imperfections and learn from mistakes rather than being overly selfcritical. Foster a mindset of self-acceptance and self-care.

10. Seek support when needed: If your child's academic pressure or performance anxiety significantly affects their well-being or academic performance, consider seeking additional support from school counselors, teachers, or mental health professionals. They can provide guidance and interventions tailored to your child's needs.

Remember, it's important to support your child's holistic development rather than solely focusing on academic achievements. Use CBT strategies to promote a balanced perspective, develop resilience, and foster a positive mindset. Encourage them to develop a love for learning and to find joy in the process of academic growth.

8.4 Supporting Children with Emotional or Behavioral Disorders

Supporting children with emotional or behavioral disorders can be challenging but crucial for their well-being. Here are some strategies to help you as a parent:

1. Educate yourself: Learn about your child's specific emotional or behavioral disorder. Understand the symptoms, triggers, and potential challenges associated with their condition. This knowledge will help you provide effective support and advocate for their needs.

2. Seek professional guidance: Consult with mental health professionals, such as therapists, psychologists, or psychiatrists, who specialize in working with children with emotional or behavioral disorders. They can provide guidance, assessments, and evidence-based interventions tailored to your child's specific needs.

3. Establish routines and structure: Children with emotional or behavioral disorders often benefit from predictable routines and structure. Create a consistent daily schedule for activities, meals, and sleep. This provides a sense of stability and can help manage anxiety and stress.

4. Provide clear and consistent expectations: Communicate behavioral expectations to your child. Use simple and concise language, and reinforce those expectations consistently. This helps them understand boundaries and develop self-regulation skills.

5. Use positive reinforcement: Implement a system of positive reinforcement to encourage desired behaviors. Praise and reward your child when they exhibit positive behaviors or makes progress. This strengthens their motivation and self-esteem.

6.   Teach emotional regulation skills: Help your child develop emotional regulation skills. Teach them strategies for identifying and expressing their emotions in healthy ways, such as deep breathing, taking breaks, or engaging in calming activities. Model these techniques and practice them together.

7.   Foster open communication: Create a safe and non-judgmental environment where your child feels comfortable expressing their thoughts and feelings. Encourage them to share their experiences, fears, and concerns. Active listening and empathy are key in fostering open communication.

8.   Collaborate with educators and professionals: Maintain open lines of communication with your child's teachers, school counselors, and therapists. Share relevant information about your child's emotional or behavioral disorder and work together to develop appropriate strategies and accommodations at school.

9. Provide social support: Help your child build positive social connections. Encourage them to engage in activities or join clubs where they can interact with peers who share similar interests.

Foster opportunities for socialization and guide building and maintaining healthy relationships.

10. Practice self-care: Caring for a child with emotional or behavioral disorders can be demanding. Make self-care a priority to ensure you have the energy and emotional resources to support your child effectively. Take breaks, seek support from loved ones, and engage in activities that rejuvenate you.

Remember, every child is unique, and strategies may need to be tailored to their specific needs. Be patient, understanding, and flexible as you navigate the challenges together. Your unconditional love, support, and advocacy can make a significant difference in your child's wellbeing and development.

Conclusion:

In conclusion, embracing the power of Cognitive Behavioral Therapy (CBT) in parenting can have a profound impact on your relationship with your children. Here's a recap of key takeaways: 1. Promoting independence and responsibility: Use CBT strategies to empower your children to take ownership of their actions and decisions, fostering independence and responsibility. 2. Nurturing self-esteem and positive self-image: Employ CBT techniques to help your children develop healthy self-esteem, positive self-image, and a resilient mindset.

3. Bonding through play: Strengthen the parentchild relationship through play by being fully present, following their lead, and incorporating cooperative and imaginative play.

4.   Managing behavioral issues and tantrums: Utilize CBT strategies to manage behavioral issues by staying calm, setting boundaries, using positive reinforcement, and teaching problem-solving skills.

5.   Addressing anxiety and stress: Address anxiety and stress in children by creating a safe environment, promoting open communication, teaching relaxation techniques, and encouraging self-care.

6.   Dealing with academic pressure and performance anxiety: Use CBT strategies to address academic pressure and performance anxiety by reframing negative thoughts, setting realistic expectations, promoting a growth mindset, and fostering effective study skills.

7.   Supporting children with emotional or behavioral disorders: Support children with emotional or behavioral disorders through education, seeking professional guidance, establishing routines, providing clear expectations, and teaching emotional regulation skills.

As a parent, remember that growth is an ongoing process. Embrace the opportunity for continuous learning and personal growth as you navigate the challenges of parenting. Seek support when needed, whether from professionals, support groups, or trusted individuals in your life.

By applying CBT strategies in your parenting approach, you can build lifelong bonds with your children. Emphasize love, empathy, and understanding in your interactions. Celebrate their unique qualities and support their journey of self-discovery and personal growth.

Your commitment to their well-being and development will create a lasting impact, shaping them into confident, resilient, and compassionate individuals. Embrace the power of CBT in your parenting journey, and enjoy the transformative experiences that come with it.

I have a Request

Dear Reader,

I trust that you found "The essential CBT guide for parents; Building Strong Bonds using Evidence Based Strategies and Tools for Meaningful Parent Child Relationships through CBT " to be a valuable resource in your quest to navigate and overcome the challenges of parenthood. I hold your opinion in high regard and kindly request a moment of your time to share your thoughts.

Your feedback carries substantial weight and can significantly assist others in making informed decisions regarding this book. Whether you found the content captivating, the techniques practical, or the information well-articulated, your insights have the potential to motivate and steer fellow readers.

If you can spare a few minutes, I would be deeply appreciative if you could compose a review on platforms like Goodreads, Amazon, or any other book review website.

Your candid evaluations will not only aid me in enhancing my work but also empower me to keep creating valuable resources for individuals like yourself. Thank you for embarking on this journey with me, and I eagerly await your reflections on "The essential CBT guide for parents; Building Strong Bonds using Evidence Based Strategies and Tools for Meaningful Parent Child Relationships through CBT" Your support is genuinely cherished!

Warm regards,
Maxine D Condon

ADDITIONAL RESOURCES

Dear Reader,

I am delighted to connect with you once again.
First and foremost, I want to express my sincere gratitude for your unwavering support and interest in "The essential CBT guide for parents; Building Strong Bonds using Evidence Based Strategies and Tools for Meaningful Parent Child Relationships through CBT." If you found this book valuable and are eager for more enriching content, I'd like to extend a recommendation for some of my other literary works and series that may captivate your interest;

1. COGNITIVE BEHAVIORAL THERAPY MANUAL FOR GRIEF; Empowering Your Mind to Heal and recover from grief and loss through CBT

2. THE DBT ANGER MANAGEMENT WORKBOOK FOR TEENS; Unlock Your Inner Calm: Proven Strategies to Help Teens Manage Anger & Stress with DBT

3. DBT SKILLS WORKBOOK FOR OCD; A Comprehensive Cognitive Behavioral Therapy Workbook for OCD Treatment

4. DBT skills workbook for borderline personality disorder (BPD); The Essential BPD survival Guide to Achieving Emotional Stability with DBT

5. DBT WORKBOOK FOR DEPRESSION AND ANXIETY; A Step-by-Step Guide to Overcoming Depression and Anxiety with DBT.

6. CBT FOR WEIGHT LOSS; A Workbook for overweight Adults

7. CBT FOR PAIN MANAGEMENT; A Workbook on how to use CBT to manage pain reduce stress and improve your quality of life

8. DBT SKILLS WORKBOOK FOR TEENS; A Practical Guide to Developing Emotional Resilience and Coping in Difficult Times for teenagers

9. Acceptance and Commitment Therapy Manual for Addiction Recovery; Embrace a life of Freedom and Fulfilment

10. A COGNITIVE BEHAVIORAL THERAPY (CBT) APPROACH FOR PSYCHOSIS; A Comprehensive Guide to Managing Symptoms and Improving Quality of Life

To explore this assortment of books and more, I invite you to visit my Author Central page on Amazon. There, you will discover a comprehensive collection of my writings, including additional series and resources that might intrigue you.

Feel free to scan the QR code below or simply click the link to access my Author Central page.

https://amazon.com/author/maxinedcondon

Your continued support means the world to me and I am committed to providing you with valuable information and inspiration on your journey to a joyful and empowered living.

Thank you for being a part of this community and I hope my books continue to bring you joy and empowerment.

Warm regards,
Maxine D Condon

Made in United States
Troutdale, OR
04/18/2024

19272899R00086